Nelson International Comprehension Year Student's Book

GW01551141

Contents

OXFORD
UNIVERSITY PRESS

SCOPE AND SEQUENCE YEAR 5

TEXT	THINK ABOUT	VOCABULARY
Unit 1 Fantastic Mr Fox modern fiction	literal comprehension multiple choice	plurals definitions
Unit 2 Book covers	literal comprehension sentence writing	'non' words
Unit 3 The Wind poetry	literal comprehension sentence writing	rhyming words verbs
Unit 4 The Big Match modern fiction	literal comprehension sentence writing	defining phrases
Unit 5 Discovering Dinosaurs information	literal comprehension multiple choice	expressions definitions
Unit 6 Nowhere to play poetry	literal comprehension sentence writing	definitions
Unit 7 Hansel and Gretel traditional tale	literal comprehension sentence writing	verbs
Unit 8 Snakes factual writing	literal comprehension cloze	definitions
Unit 9 Wagon Train to California 1st person narrative	literal comprehension sentence writing	defining phrases
Unit 10 Why Tigers have Stripes Traditional story	literal comprehension sentence writing	'qu' words
Unit 11 Person Power poetry	literal comprehension multiple choice	rhyming words adjectives
Unit 12 Pie charts diagram	literal comprehension sentence writing	plurals
Unit 13 Hills End modern fiction	literal comprehension sentence writing	definitions adverbs
Unit 14 Timetables diagram	literal comprehension sentence writing	compound words
Unit 15 The Story of Gelert traditional tale	literal comprehension sentence writing	defining phrases verbs

TALK ABOUT	EXTRA
inferential comprehension	story ending
inferential comprehension	creating a book cover summary
inferential comprehension	personal response
inferential comprehension	story ending & personal response
inferential comprehension	research & factual writing
inferential comprehension	descriptive/ personal writing
inferential comprehension	conversation
inferential comprehension	research & factual writing
inferential comprehension	personal response
inferential comprehension	writing as a character
inferential writing comprehension	personal response
reading diagrams	creating a pie chart
inferential comprehension	writing as a character
using a timetable	creating a timetable
inferential comprehension	writing as a character

Fantastic Mr Fox

Three nasty, mean farmers live in a valley. Mr Boggis is a chicken farmer.
Mr Bunce is a duck and goose farmer. Mr Bean is a turkey and apple farmer.
They are very angry because Mr Fox steals from them to feed his family.
Mr Bean has a plan to get rid of Mr Fox. He suggests that the three farmers
hide outside Mr Fox's hole and shoot him when he comes out.

'Well, my darling,' said Mr Fox. 'What shall it be tonight?'

'I think we'll have duck tonight,' said Mrs Fox. 'Bring two fat ducks, if you please. One for you and me, and one for the children.'

'Ducks it shall be!' said Mr Fox. 'Bunce's best!'

'Now do be careful,' said Mrs Fox.

'My darling,' said Mr Fox, 'I can smell those goons a mile away. I can even smell one from the other. Boggis gives off a filthy stink of rotten chicken-skins. Bunce reeks of goose-livers, and as for Bean, the fumes of the apple cider hang around him like poisonous gases.'

'Yes, but don't get careless,' said Mrs Fox. 'You know they'll be waiting for you, all three of them.'

'Don't worry about me,' said Mr Fox. 'I'll see you later.'

But Mr Fox would not have been quite so cocky had he known exactly where the three farmers were waiting at that moment. They were outside the entrance to the hole, each one crouching behind a tree with his gun loaded. And what is more, they had chosen their positions very carefully, making sure that the wind was not blowing from them towards the fox's hole. In fact, it was blowing in the opposite direction. There was no chance of them being 'smelled out'.

Mr Fox crept up the dark tunnel to the mouth of his hole. He poked his long handsome face out into the night air and sniffed once.

He moved an inch or two forward and stopped. He sniffed again. He was always especially careful when coming out of his hole.

He inched forward a little more. The front half of his body was now in the open.

His black nose twitched from side to side, sniffing and sniffing for the scent of danger. He found none, and he was just about to go trotting forward into the wood when he heard or thought he heard a tiny noise, a soft rustling sound, as though someone had moved a foot ever so gently through a patch of dry leaves.

Mr Fox flattened his body against the ground and lay very still, his ears pricked. He waited a long time, but he heard nothing more.

'It must have been a field-mouse,' he told himself, 'or some other small animal. '

He crept a little further out of the hole…then further still. He was almost right out in the open now. He took a last careful look around. The wood was murky and very still. Somewhere in the sky, the moon was shining.

Roald Dahl

A Think about

Copy each sentence. Write the correct ending.

1 For dinner that night, Mrs Fox wanted _____

  goose.   duck.   turkey.

2 Mr Fox could tell the farmers apart because of the way they

  _____

  looked.   walked.   smelled.

3 Mr Fox crept up the dark tunnel and poked out _____
  his face.   his tail.   his paws.

4 Mr Fox heard _____
  a cough.   a rustle.   a sneeze.

5 He thought the sound was made by _____
  the farmers.   Mrs Fox.   a small animal.

B Vocabulary

1 | Fox**es** is the plural of fox.

  Plural means more than one.

Write the plural of these words.
a box   b inch   c gas   d bush

2 Write the words in the story that mean:

a idiots   begins with **g**

b smells strongly   begins with **r**

c confident   begins with **c**

d more than usual   begins with **e**

e dark and gloomy   begins with **m**

C Talk about

1 What does Mrs Fox say that shows she was worried about Mr Fox going hunting?

2 How does Mr Fox feel about the three farmers?

3 What do you imagine the three farmers were thinking about as they waited for Mr Fox?

4 Why did Mr Fox take such a long time to come out of his hole?

5 Mr Fox takes food from the farmers. Is this stealing? Can an animal 'steal' like a person can?

6 Are the farmers right to try to shoot Mr Fox?

D Extra

How do you think the story ends?

Do the farmers shoot Mr Fox?

Does he get away? How does he do this?

Write an ending for the story.

Look at these book covers.

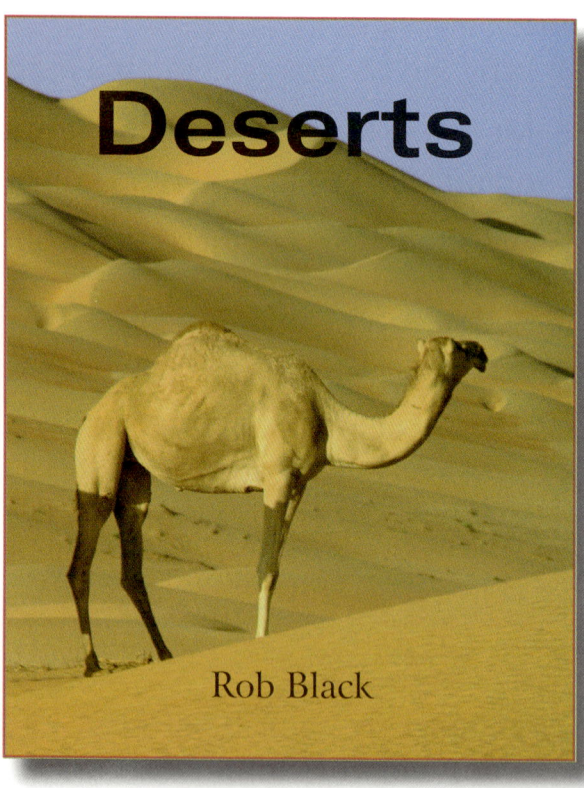

This is a fiction book.
Fiction books tell stories.

This is a non-fiction book.
Non-fiction books give us
facts and information.

A Think about

1 What is the title of the fiction book?

2 Who wrote it?

3 What is the title of the non-fiction book?

4 Who wrote it?

B Vocabulary

When we use the word **non** in front of another word,
we mean **not**.

e.g.   non-fiction   =   not fiction

Complete the sentences.

1 If a pan is non-stick it means that _____.

2 If something in nonsense we mean that _____.

3 If something is non-stop we mean that _____.

4 If it is a non-uniform day in school we mean that _____.

5 If a disease in non-infectious we mean that _____.

C Talk about

Look at these book covers.

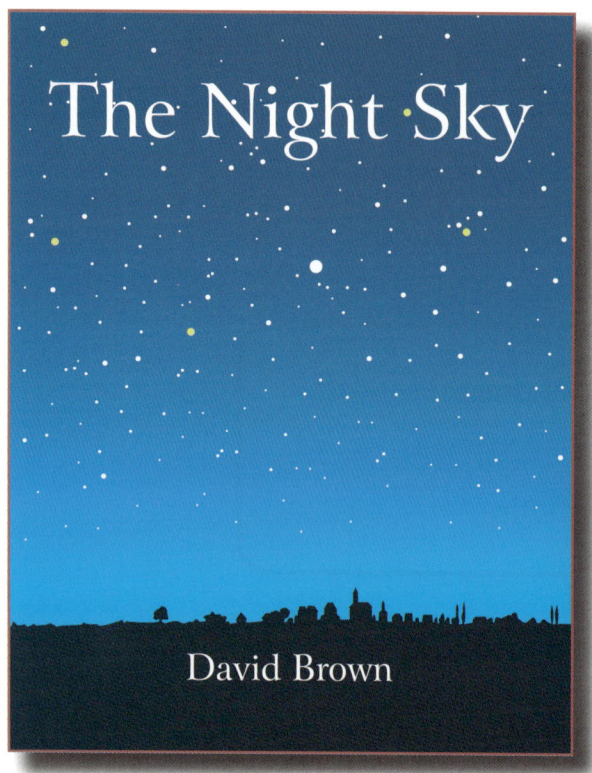

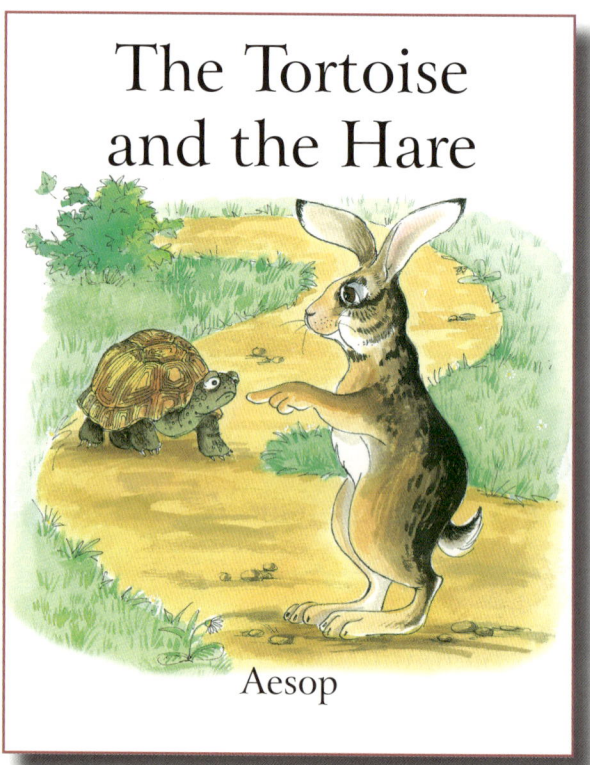

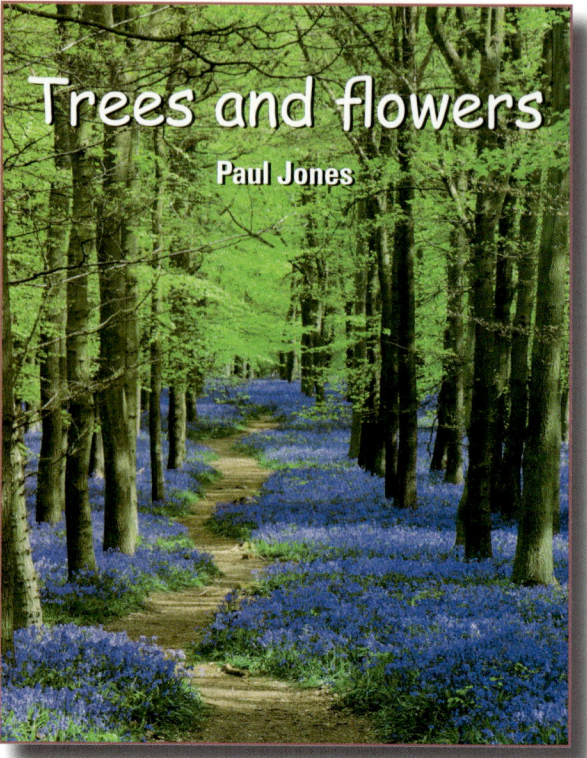

1 Which book would you read to learn about lions and tigers?

2 Who is the author of that book?

3 Which of the four books is fiction?

4 Who is the author of that book?

5 Which book would you read to learn about the stars?

6 Which book did Paul Jones write?

D Extra

Think of a fiction or non-fiction book you have read.

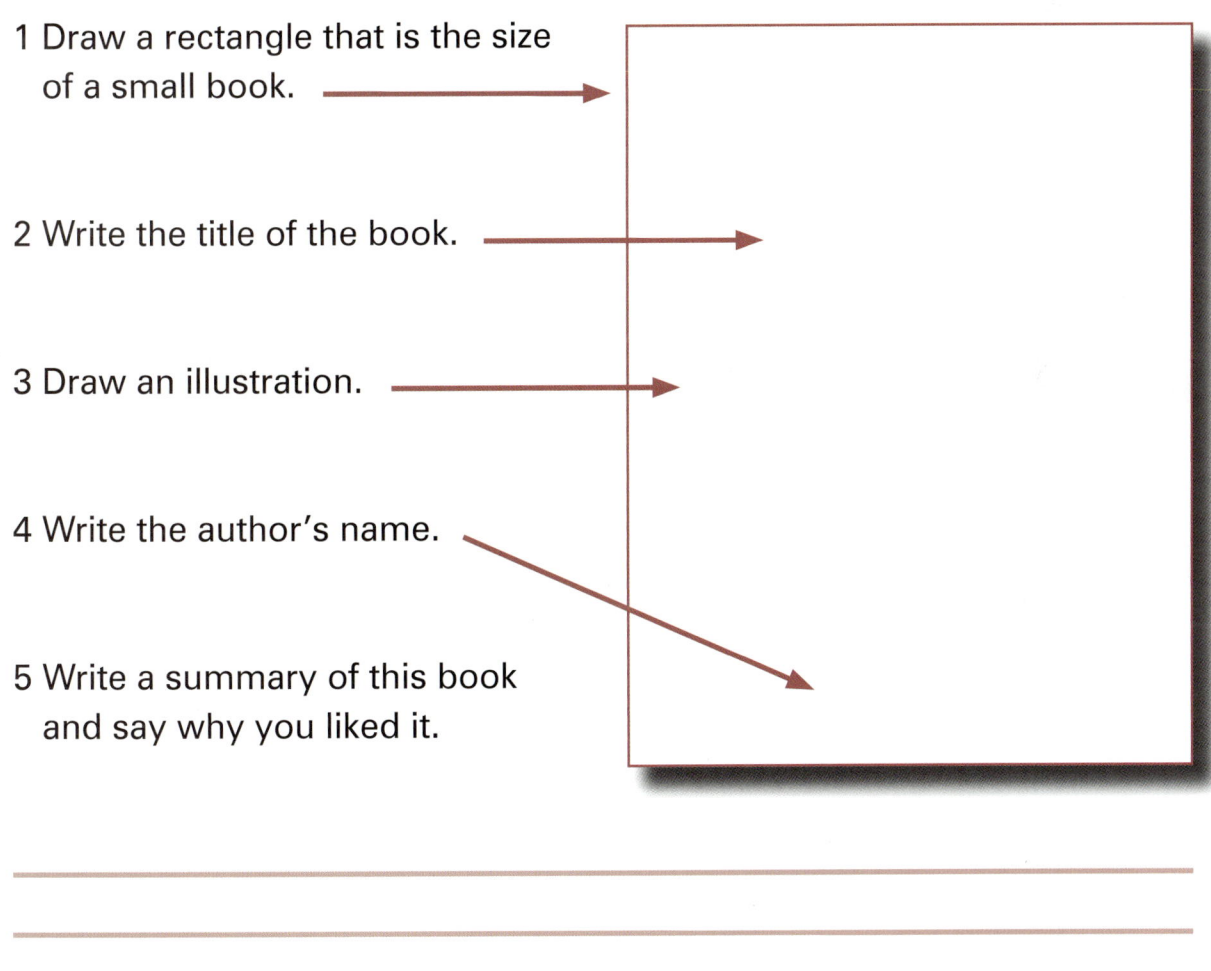

1 Draw a rectangle that is the size of a small book.

2 Write the title of the book.

3 Draw an illustration.

4 Write the author's name.

5 Write a summary of this book and say why you liked it.

The wind is a wolf
That sniffs at doors
And rattles windows
With his paws.

Hidden in the night,
He rushes round
The lock-up house
Making angry sounds.

He leaps on the roof
And tries to drive
Away the house
And everything inside.

Tired the next morning,
The wind's still there
Snatching at paper
And ruffling your hair.

He quietens down and in the end
You hardly notice him go
Whispering down the road
To find another place to blow.

Stanley Cook

A Think about

Write a sentence to answer each question.

1 What animal is the wind like?

2 What does the wind do to the windows?

3 What sort of sounds does the wind make?

4 What does the wind do to people's hair?

5 Where is the wind going at the end of the poem?

B Vocabulary

1 Copy this list of words. Find a word in the poem that rhymes with each one.

    a   doors

    b   round

    c   there

    d   go

2 Add a rhyming word of your own to each list.

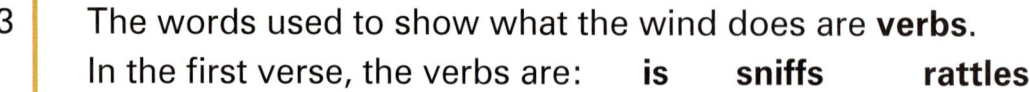

3   The words used to show what the wind does are **verbs**.
In the first verse, the verbs are: **is**   **sniffs**   **rattles**

    Find the verbs in the other verses.

C Talk about

1 Why do you think that the poet says that the wind is 'a wolf'?

2 In what ways does the wind behave like a wolf?

3 Why does the wind not blow so hard in the morning?

4 Why does the poet say that the wind goes 'whispering' away in the morning?

5 Do you like the poem? Say why or why not.

D Extra

Imagine you are at home with your family.

It is night time and the wind begins to blow.

It gets stronger and stronger.

- Write about the noise you hear.

  What is the wind blowing about outside?

  What noises does it make as it blows against the house?

- Write about how you feel.

  Are you frightened?

  Do you feel safe in the house?

The Big Match

Chris is given a chance to be the goalkeeper in the Danebridge Primary School football team. They are playing a cup match against Shenby school. Towards the end of the match, Danebridge are leading 3 – 2 when disaster strikes.

The cup match became an exciting end-to-end battle as the teams threw everything that they had left at each other and both goals survived narrow squeaks. Time was rapidly running out, though, for Shenby when they forced Chris to tip the ball round the post for yet another corner and Tim signalled everyone back into the penalty area to protect their slender lead.

The winger played a neat short-corner before whipping the ball across into the box through a great ruck of bodies. It suddenly loomed up in front of Duggan who reacted by blocking it with his hands in panic before a Shenby player could get at it.

As he booted it away, the Shenby team and their supporters were already loudly demanding a penalty for hand-ball and he slumped to the ground in distress.

'It was an accident, I didn't mean to,' he pleaded, shaking his head and failing to find an excuse for his stunned team-mates. 'I don't know why I did it – it just happened…'

The referee had no choice, however, but to award a penalty kick and all their hard work seemed to be wasted. Duggan's eyes were not the only ones to be fixed on the goalkeeper Chris in the desperate hope that he could yet somehow rescue the situation.

John Duggan wished he had not said so many nasty things to him, but it was too late to make up for that now. At least the kid was a good keeper, he had to admit to himself in consolation. Chris had certainly proved that to everyone, whatever happened in these next few minutes.

He settled himself on the goal-line, surprised that he felt quite calm considering that everything was at stake and it all seemed to depend on him. He had never faced a proper penalty like this before and he was not really sure what to expect. The goal around him looked massive and he stared instead at the ball, noticing all the dirty marks on it as it sat perched up on the muddy penalty spot a few metres directly in front of him.

The spectators grew hushed in anticipation of the duel, the final shoot-out, and some of the players grouped around the edge of the area hardly daring to watch as the Shenby captain prepared to run in to take the penalty.

Rob Child

A Think about

Copy the sentences that are true.

1 Chris was the goalkeeper for Shenby School.
2 Duggan touched the ball with his hand.
3 Duggan thought that Chris was no good as a goalkeeper.
4 Chris was very nervous about the penalty shot.
5 The Shenby captain took the penalty shot.

B Vocabulary

In your own words write what these phrases in the story mean:

1 end-to-end battle
2 narrow squeaks
3 slender lead
4 ruck of bodies
5 in distress
6 had no choice
7 rescue the situation
8 anticipation of the duel

C Talk about

1 How do you know that Duggan was really upset to have given away a penalty?

2 What does the author mean when he says that 'all their hard work seemed to be wasted'?

3 How do you know that Duggan and Chris were not best friends?

4 Why do you think that Chris was 'surprised that he felt quite calm' just before the penalty was going to be taken?

5 How would you have felt if you were Chris? Say why you would feel like this.

6 Why do you think some of the players 'hardly dared to watch'?

D Extra

1 Does Chris save the penalty?

Does the Shenby captain score?

Write an ending for the story.

2 Chris's favourite sport was football.

Write about your favourite sport.

Say why you like it.

If you don't like any sport, write about why you dislike it.

Discovering dinosaurs

Dinosaur remains have been found in all continents except Antarctica. The position of these sites depends on the age and type of the rocks, and a lucky discovery by a fossil collector! New dinosaur sites are discovered every year, and there are clearly many more to be found.

The first dinosaur remains were collected in the 19th century in England, often in old quarries, or at the foot of sea cliffs. Dinosaur fossils were soon discovered in other parts of Europe and North America. During the 20th century, large dinosaur collecting expeditions have gone to all corners of the world, and hundreds of tonnes of huge bones have come to light.

Between 1895 and 1905, the millionaire, Andrew Carnegie, spent 25 million dollars on large fossil-collecting trips in Western America. A complete skeleton of Diplodocus was found for him in 1899, and Carnegie had life-size casts made and sent to all the leading museums in the world. One of his collectors, Earl Douglass, found a remarkable deposit of dinosaur skeletons in Colorado, and in 1925 this was named the Dinosaur National Monument.

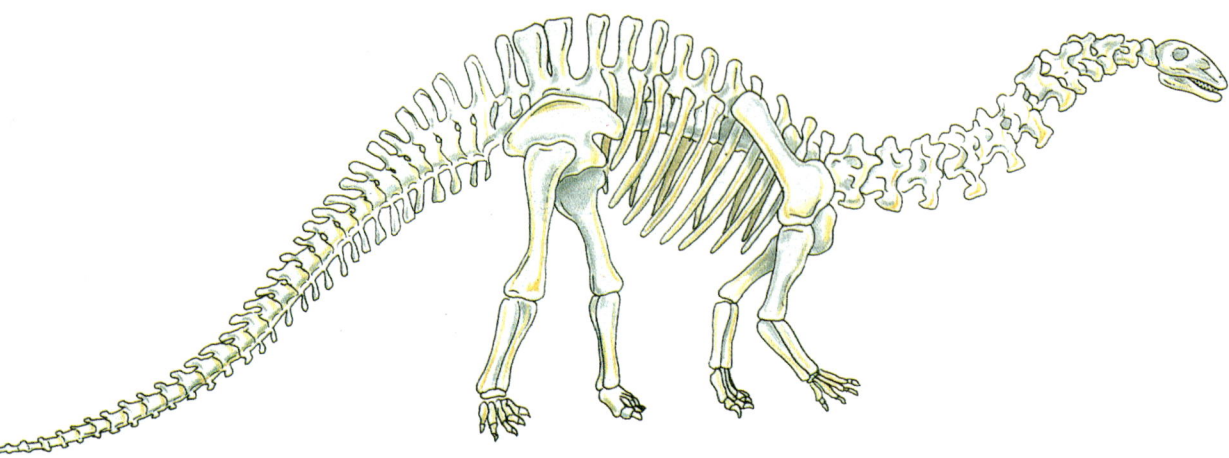

Similar huge dinosaur deposits were discovered in the last century along the Red Deer River in Alberta, Canada. Barnum Brown and Charles Sternberg led two teams which collected hundreds of specimens between 1900 and 1920.

A huge dinosaur collecting expedition began in 1907 in Tanzania (then German East Africa). The German geologist, Werner Janensch, worked there for four years and sent 250 tonnes of bones back to Berlin, including those of the giant Brachiosaurus.

More recent finds have been made in Mongolia, China, Australia, South America, and in 1988 in the Sahara Desert.

A Think about

Copy the sentences. Choose the best ending.

1 Dinosaurs have been found all over the world except for
   New Zealand.
   Antarctica.
   South America.

2 The man who spent 25 million dollars looking for dinosaurs was
   Barnum Brown.
   Werner Janensch.
   Andrew Carnegie.

3 The complete skeleton Carnegie found was of

Diplodocus.

Brachiosaurus.

Triceratops.

4 Brown and Sternberg collected dinosaur remains between

1895 and 1905.

1899 and 1915.

1900 and 1920.

5 The German geologist, Werner Janensch, worked in

Tanzania.

Colorado.

Alberta.

B Vocabulary

1 Find these expressions in the passage and write in your own words what you think they mean.

a   all corners of the world

b   come to light

c   leading museums

d   more recent finds

2 Look up each word in your dictionary and write its meaning.

a   continent

b   fossil

c   expedition

d   geologist

C Talk about

1 Why do you think some discoveries by fossil collectors are 'lucky'?

2 Why do you think that the first fossils were found in old quarries or at the foot of sea cliffs?

3 Why do you think people keep looking for dinosaur fossils?

4 Look on a map of the world and find all the places where dinosaur fossils have been found. What does that tell you about where dinosaurs lived?

D Extra

Triceratops

Tyrannosaurus

Iguanadon

Stegosaurus

Choose one of these dinosaurs to research. Try to find out:

1 How long was it?

2 How tall did it grow?

3 What did it eat?

4 Where in the world have its fossils been discovered?

Unit 6 Nowhere to play

Nowhere to play;
Backstreets and alleyways,
Car parks and main roads;
Noise, dirt and danger all day.
Same old smells;
Exhaust, cars,
People, rubbish,
No smells of earth after rain.
Same old noises;
Rush of traffic,
Cops on their way;
'Where's the ice-cream man today?'

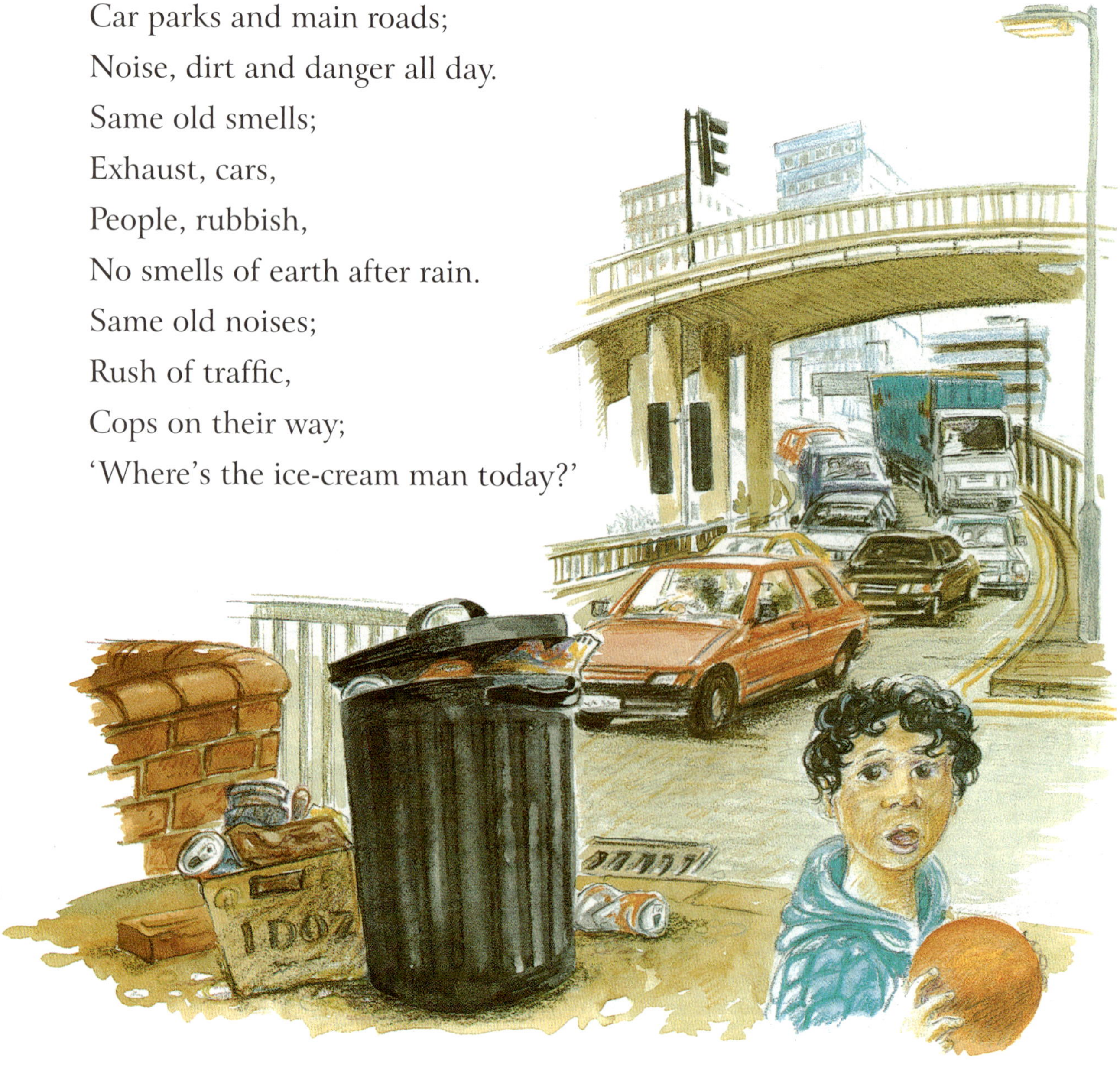

No new sensations;
Same hard pavements,
No mud to explore.
No pebbles, no pieces of wood to arrange.
Big buildings,
Big buses, big people;
No bee or buttercup,
No ants on their way.
No green grass, just concrete,
No thrush song, just sirens.
Seasons passing unnoticed;
Nowhere to play –
'What's on telly today?'

Nicola Tyson

A Think about

Write a sentence to answer each question.

1 Name two places where the poet thinks it is dangerous, dirty and noisy to play.

2 What can the poet smell in these places?

3 What smell is missing?

4 What big things are all around?

5 Name three things that the poet cannot find around her.

B Vocabulary

Which word in the poem means:

1 odours   It begins with **s**

2 sounds   It begins with **n**

3 police officers It begins with **c**

4 find out about   It begins with **e**

5 warning hooters It begins with **s**

6 not seen   It begins with **u**

C Talk about

1 How do you think the poet feels about her surroundings?

2 Where do you think the poet would like to play?

3 What do you think she means when she writes 'No new sensations'?

4 Why do you think the seasons 'pass unnoticed'?

5 Why does the poet ask, 'What's on telly today?' ?

D Extra

Where do you usually play? Is it a place you like or dislike?

Write a description of the place where you play and say why you like it or dislike it. The pictures will help you.

Hansel and Grethel

Hansel and Grethel were the children of a poor woodman and his selfish wife. When there was no food to eat, the wife told her husband to take the children into the forest and leave them there. They found their way back by following a trail of stones Hansel had dropped on the way. The selfish wife said they must take the children deeper into the wood. Hansel had a small piece of bread with him and he left a trail of breadcrumbs for them to follow home.

There they were told to sit down by a large fire and go to sleep. The woodman and his wife said they would come along in the evening and take them home.

In the afternoon, Hansel shared Grethel's bread because he had dropped all his along the path. The day passed away and the evening passed away too, but no one came to fetch the poor children. Hansel comforted Grethel and said, 'Wait until the moon rises and then I shall be able to see the crumbs of bread that I dropped. They will show us the way home.'

The moon rose, but when Hansel looked for the crumbs they were gone! Hundreds of little birds in the wood had found them and eaten them. Hansel, however, set out to try and find his way home. Soon they lost their way, but they went on through the night and all the next day. When they were too tired to go any further, they lay down and slept.

The next day they went on as before but still they did not come to the end of the wood. They were as hungry as could be for they had had nothing to eat.

In the afternoon of the third day, they came to a strange little hut made of bread, with a roof of cake and windows of barley-sugar. 'Now we will sit and eat until we have had enough,' said Hansel. 'I will eat off the roof for my share. You eat the windows, Grethel. They will be nice and sweet for you.' Whilst Grethel broke a piece of barley-sugar, a pretty voice called softly from the hut.

'Tip, tap! Who goes there?'

The children answered, 'The wind, the wind, that blows through the air!' They went on eating. Now Grethel had broken out a round pane of the window for herself, and Hansel had torn off a large piece of cake from the roof. Suddenly, the door opened and a little old lady came gliding out. Hansel and Grethel were so frightened that they let fall what they had in their hands. The dear old lady nodded to them and said, 'Dear children, where have you been wandering about? Come in with me and you shall have something good to eat.'

Adapted from the Brothers Grimm

A Think about

Write a sentence to answer each question.

1 Why did Hansel have to share Grethel's bread?

2 How was Hansel going to find his way home?

3 What happened to the crumbs?

4 What happened on the afternoon of the third day?

5 What happened at the little hut that frightened Hansel and Grethel?

B Vocabulary

Copy and complete the chart. You will find the answers in the story.

What will happen in the **future**?	What happened in the **past**?
a I will rise.	I rose.
b I will sleep.	I _____.
c I will come.	I _____.
d I will find.	I _____.
e I will lose.	I _____.
f I will go.	I _____.
g I will break.	I _____.

C Talk about

1 What do you think of Hansel and Grethel's parents for leaving them in the wood?

2 How do you think Hansel and Grethel were feeling as 'the evening passed away'?

3 Why do you think Hansel didn't take pebbles with him the second time?

4 Do you think that Hansel and Grethel should have broken off pieces of the hut to eat? Say why or why not.

5 If you had been Hansel or Grethel, would you have gone into the lady's hut? Say why or why not.

D Extra

The selfish wife wants her husband to take Hansel and Grethel into the wood and leave them there.

Their father does not want to do this.

Write the conversation between the selfish wife and her husband.

She has to say things that will persuade him to do as she wants.

He has to find good reasons for not doing what she wants.

Take the children into the wood and leave them there!

I don't want to do that.

Snakes are reptiles. They have no legs but many ribs that help them to slide along the ground. They have no ears and no eyelids. Like all other reptiles, they are cold-blooded. Their temperature is controlled by their environment and they dislike very hot and very cold temperatures.

All snakes hunt. Poisonous snakes, such as cobras, poison their prey by biting them with their fangs. Constrictor snakes, such as pythons, coil themselves around their prey. Snakes that do not kill their prey by poison or constricting, usually snatch it up and swallow it whole. Their mouths and jaws will stretch and open very wide.

There are nearly 2,500 different types of snakes in the world. Only 200 types of snake are dangerous enough to kill people. The biggest, most deadly snake is the king cobra. The puff adder, which inhabits Africa, is also very dangerous.

king cobra

puff adder

A Think about

Copy these sentences. Fill in the missing words.

1 Snakes move along the ground using their _____.

2 Snakes have no _____, no _____ and no _____.

3 Snakes _____ for their food.

4 There are 200 types of _____ snakes that can kill people.

5 The _____ _____ lives in Africa.

B Vocabulary

Explain the meaning of each word.

1 reptile   2 environment   3 prey

4 fangs   5 deadly   6 inhabits

C Talk about

1 What do all reptiles have in common?

2 How can some snakes swallow what they catch in one go?

3 Which is the biggest, deadliest snake?

4 Many people are frightened of snakes. Why do you think people are frightened?

D Extra

Look at the photographs of these snakes.

grass snake

boa constrictor

Indian python

black mamba

1 Find an information book about snakes or go on the web.

Choose one of the snakes in the photographs and answer these questions.

a How long does it grow?

b What does it feed on?

c Where does it live?

2 Find out any other information about your snake and write a paragraph about it.

Wagon train to California

March 22, 1847

My name is Lucy Bennet and I am 15 years old. My parents, my brother, my baby sister and I are setting out for California. Father and Mother are excited, though they say it will be a long, difficult journey. My brother and I are sorry to leave our friends in Indiana, but we've heard California is a wonderful place. They say the sun always shines there and the fruit grows wild for the picking.

We are waiting in Independence, Missouri, for the rest of our wagon train to gather. Many of our aunts, uncles and cousins will join us. Going west seems to be a family affair, as there are many others awaiting kin.

April 13, 1847

At last the snows have melted and the roads are hard enough for us to travel. Our family has arrived safely and our supplies are securely packed in the wagon. Going west is expensive and calls for careful planning. Father says our wagon and the oxen and mules to pull it cost nearly $400. Inside the wagon we have 200 pounds of flour, 150 pounds of bacon, 10 pounds of coffee, 20 pounds of sugar and 10 pounds of salt. We also have a good supply off chipped beef, rice, tea, beans, dried fruit, baking soda and vinegar. Then, of course, we carry the usual cooking pots, tools, and supplies of powder, lead and shot for Father's rifles. All this is in addition to the household and farming supplies we'll need in California and a small amount of cash for emergencies. In all, we had to save nearly $1,000 for the journey.

A Think about

Write a sentence to answer each question.

1 Where were the Bennett family going?

2 Where were they travelling from?

3 What form of transport were they going to use?

4 How much was the journey costing?

B Vocabulary

Explain the meaning of each of these words in the story.

1 wonderful

2 kin

3 securely

4 expensive

5 in addition

6 emergencies

C Talk about

1 Why do you think they needed so much food?

2 Why do you think Father might need rifles?

3 What do you think the roads were like?

4 How does Lucy feel about the journey?

5 How would you have felt about the journey?

D Extra

Lucy Bennett wrote about her experiences in a diary.

She recorded:

- facts   –   the things that happened
- feelings   –   how she felt about her experiences

Choose one of the following and write about what actually happened and how you felt.

1 My best day at school

2 My worst day at school

3 A funny thing happened to me…

This is a story from Thailand about Tah-toh, the basket weaver and the tiger that wanted to eat him. Tah-toh persuades the tiger that a great flood is coming and he can be saved if he lets the basket weaver tie him to a tree.

The tiger purred softly, happy as a chuckling baby, as Tah-toh wrapped the rattan strips firmly round and round the tiger's body. True to his promise, he gave no trouble at all as Tah-toh tied him tight to the top of the tallest tree…

'They say you never really know who your true friends are till you find yourself in trouble and need help,' smiled the tiger. 'Who would have believed that I, mighty tiger, would turn to you, oh skinny man, for help?'

'Ah!' sighed Tah-toh, 'Appearances can be deceptive, my grandmother always said. But, thinking of the past, Honourable Tiger, neither of us has been entirely fair in our dealings with each other. Therefore, relations between us have been far from cordial over the centuries. I, too, never dreamed that I would ever want to help one of your kind. Let's hope we've both learned something today…'

And so saying, Tah-toh gathered the rest of his rattan canes together and set off home, whistling.

The wily tiger waited patiently, tied to the top of his tree, for many days and many nights. But soon he began to grow hungry again. Hunger sharpened his wits, and it was not long before he realised that he had been tricked.

'**Whoo-oo-ah-aarg**!' he roared, shaking the tree with rage. Angrily he struggled, this way and that, trying hard to free himself from his bonds. But the more he struggled, the more deeply the rattan strips cut into him.

At long last, after twisting and turning for many days, the tiger managed to loosen his bonds and was able to climb slowly down from the tree. With each step he took, he groaned painfully…
'**Whoo-argh! Whoo-oo-argh**!'

The bands of rattan that had held him so firmly had cut deep into his skin and these cuts had turned black. And there they have remained to this day – black bands between the flame orange fur.

Beulah Candappa

A Think about

Write a sentence to answer each question.

1 Why did the tiger let Tah-toh tie him to the tree?

2 What did Tah-toh do when he had finished tying up the tiger?

3 After the tiger had been tied to the tree for 'many days and many nights', what did he realise?

4 What happened to the rattan strips as the tiger struggled to free himself?

5 What had the rattan strips done to the tiger's skin?

B Vocabulary

Copy the phrases from the story. Choose the correct meaning for each one.

1 appearances can be deceptive
      a things are always what they seem
      b things are never what they seem
      c things might not be what they seem

2 fair in our dealings with each other
      a going to the fair together
      b treating each other well
      c treating each other badly

3 far from cordial
      a unfriendly
      b very friendly
      c funny

4 sharpened his wits
      a made him cut himself
      b made him think more clearly
      c made him happy

C Talk about

1 What sort of man do you think Tah-toh was?

2 Do you think the tiger was wise or foolish? Give your reasons.

3 How do you think Tah-toh felt when he left the tiger tied to the tree?

4 What do you think the tiger thought about when he was first tied to the tree?

5 What do you think the tiger might have done, once he had escaped?

D Extra

Imagine you are the tiger and you have to explain to the other animals why you now have stripes.

You do not want to admit how foolish you have been!

Write what you would tell them.

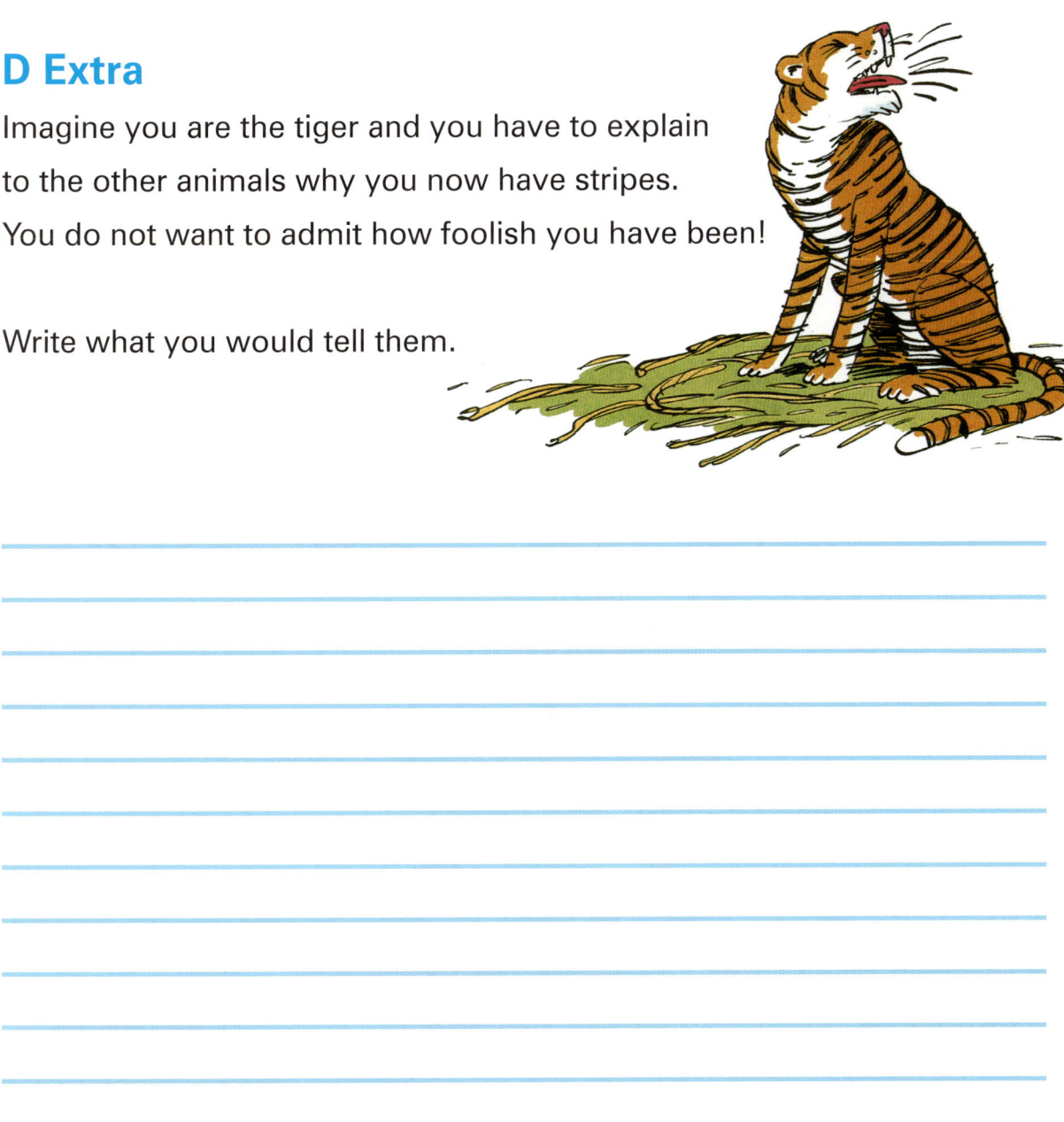

Unit 11 Person Power

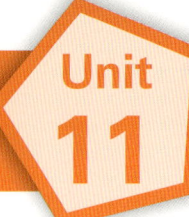

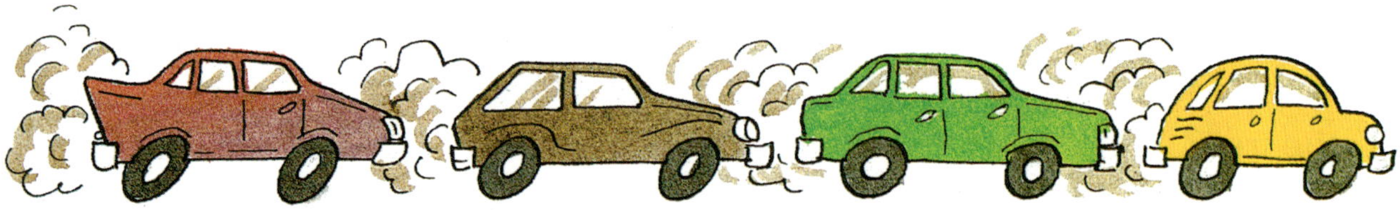

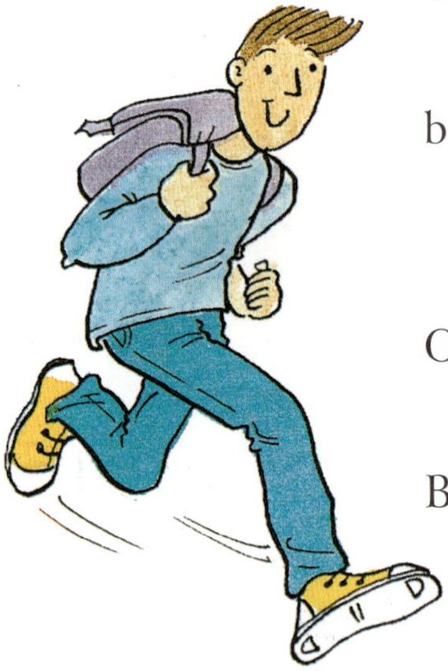

Our car drinks lead-free petrol,
it's a user-friendly fuel,
but I prefer to use my legs
to get me safe to school.

Our house is all-electric,
gas is what cookers like,
But I have lots of energy
so I pedal my red bike.

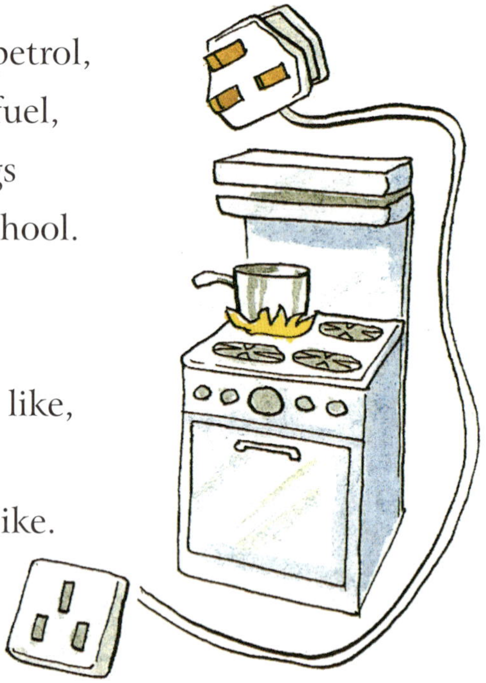

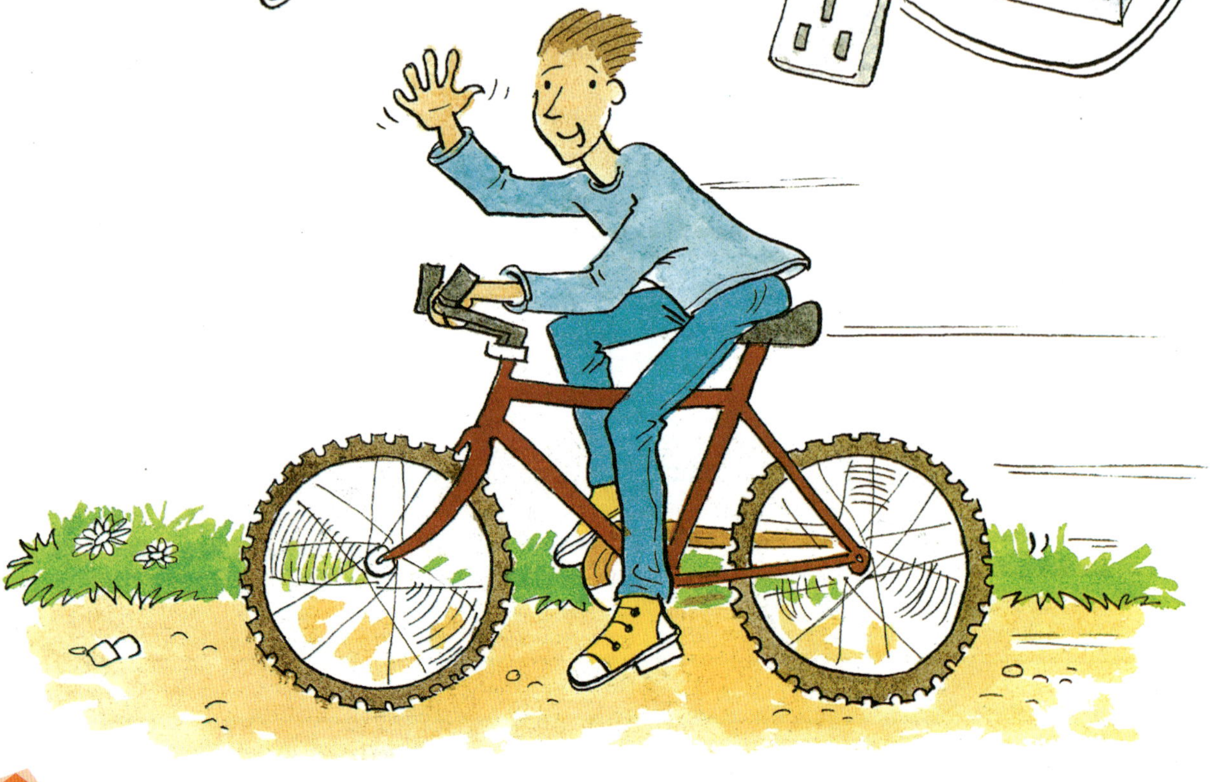

The sun heats solar panels,
    the windmill likes the breeze,
the waves have awesome power
    but I need none of these.

Just give me my strong muscles
    a skateboard, bike or skates,
and I'll use person power
    in the park to race my mates.

John Rice

A Think about

Copy the sentences. Choose the correct ending for each one.

1 The poet's car runs on _____.

    a   diesel

    b   leaded petrol

    c   lead-free petrol

2 The poet gets to school by _____.

    a   bike

    b   walking

    c   bus

3 The fuel used in the poet's house is _____.

    a   coal

    b   electricity

    c   gas

4 A windmill is powered by _____.

    a   solar panels

    b   the waves

    c   the wind

5 Person power uses _____.

    a   muscles

    b   the sun

    c   electricity

B Vocabulary

1 Write a word from the poem that rhymes with each one of these.

    a fuel   b like   c breeze   d skates

2 Find the adjectives in the poem that describes each one of these.

    a petrol   b bike   c power   d muscles

C Talk about

1 Why do you think that lead-free petrol is 'user-friendly'?

2 Where do you think solar panels would be in a house?

3 What do you think 'awesome power' means?

4 Why do you think the poet likes 'person power' instead of the other types of power?

5 Which types of power in the poem:

    a   harm the environment

    b   do not harm the environment?

D Extra

1 What do you use your 'person power' for?

Write a list of things you do in a day that need 'person power'.

Write a list of things you need other sorts of power for.

Pie charts

These are the things that John does every day.

A Think about

1 List the four main activities that John does every day.

2 Which activity do you think John spends most of his time doing?

3 Which activity do you think John spends least time doing?

4 What other activities do you think John does most days?

B Vocabulary

> Words ending in a consonant + y make their plural by changing the **y** to **i** and adding **es**.
>
>   e.g.   activity   activit**ies**
>
> Words ending in a vowel and y, just add s….
>
>   e.g.   day   day**s**

Follow the rules and write the plurals of these words.

1 lady   2 boy   3 donkey

4 valley   5 lorry   6 story

C Talk about

John's daily activities can be shown in the form of a diagram.
This diagram is called a pie chart. This pie chart is divided into 24 hours.

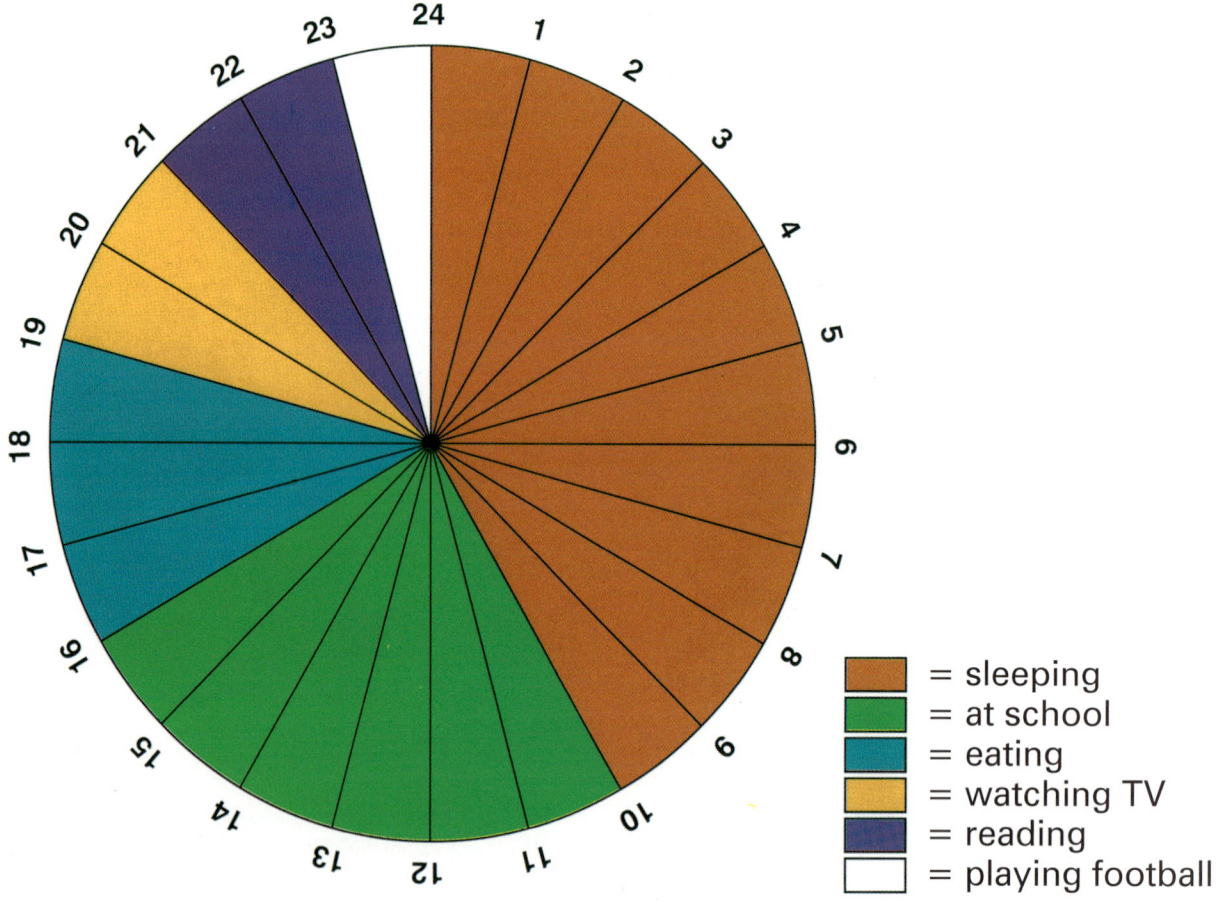

= sleeping
= at school
= eating
= watching TV
= reading
= playing football

Look carefully at the pie chart and answer the questions.

1 How many hours does John spend sleeping?

2 How many hours does John spend eating?

3 What is the total number of hours John spends reading and playing football?

4 What does John do for the fewest hours each day?

5 What does he do for most hours each day?

6 What two activities does he spend an equal amount of time on?

7 What two activities together take up 16 hours of John's day?

8 How many hours a day is John awake?

D Extra

1 Look at the following information about Mr Shaw.
Show this information in a pie chart.

8 hours

2 hours

2 hours

6 hours

1 hour

3 hours

2 hours

2 Now make a pie chart about your day.

Hills End, a village in Australia, is flooded. Most of the people who live there are away on a village picnic, but seven children and their teacher, Miss Godwin, have gone up into the mountains to look for cave paintings. The children are separated from their teacher and have to find their way back alone.

They struggled into the forest, not knowing that their crossing of the rock pan was something to be proud of. Their spirits were low. Four and a half miles of steamy, sticky, and tangled forest stretched ahead of them. When they had come the day before, they had followed the path that had been tramped by erring children for ten years. This afternoon, it was there in part only, in places washed away, in places smothered by fallen timber, and in the gullies submerged beneath streams they had never seen flow before. They leapt some of the streams, anxiously waded through some, and scouted others uphill and downhill until they found bridges of broken trees or could climb across overhanging boughs. Soon their clothes were filthy and torn.

At a quarter to four by Adrian's watch, it started raining again; steady, solid rain, but not accompanied by the violent winds and thunder of the day before. Hail didn't fall and the rain didn't roar as though its one desire was to destroy them, but in a very short time they were drenched and cold and the forest floor turned into a gloomy vault that was not at all friendly. The light was weird, as though belonging to another epoch in time or perhaps to another world. Once, from a hilltop, they caught a glimpse of the upper reaches of the bluff far behind them, with clouds swirling round it like smoke. It was low cloud such as they saw in the wet season, that sagged out of heavy skies and sometimes stayed on the mountain-tops and in the gullies for days.

They plodded on and on. They knew they were heading in the right direction, but they had long since lost the old path and were gradually forced lower into the valley towards the road, to avoid washaways and landslides. There were times they had to wallow calf-deep through mud. They had seen storm damage before, but nothing like this. Never had such a volume of wind, hail and rain struck their mountains so fiercely and in so few hours. Spread over a week, the dry land would have absorbed the rain, but too much had come too quickly, and now it was raining again.

Ivan Southall

A Think about

Write a sentence to answer each question.

1 How far did the children have to travel through the forest?

2 Explain one of the things that had happened to the path.

3 What did the children's clothes look like?

4 How was the weather different from the day before?

5 It had rained like this before. Why had so much damage been done this time?

B Vocabulary

1 Look up these words in a dictionary.

Use each one in a sentence of your own.

a err

b gully

c submerge

d anxious

e vault

f weird

g epoch

2

> Some **adverbs** tell us **how** something was done.
>
> e.g.   They… **anxiously** waded
>
>   The rain struck… **fiercely**

Use these adverbs in sentences of your own.

a dangerously   b carefully   c tiredly

d quickly   e hungrily   f violently

C Talk about

1 How do you think the children felt when they were separated from their teacher?

2 The writer says that the children's 'spirits were low'. In your own words describe how you think they were feeling.

3 Why do you think the children were anxious when they waded through some of the streams?

4 How do you think they knew that 'they were headed in the right direction'?

5 The children were 'gradually forced lower into the valley'. Why was this a dangerous place to be?

D Extra

Imagine that you are one of the children in the story.

The others are too weak to go on.

You must get down from the mountains alone and get help.

Describe the journey you make to reach the village.

Tim has just started his new school. Here is his timetable for the mornings.

	9.00 – 9.45	9.45 – 10.30		10.45 – 11.30	11.30 – 12.00
Mon	Maths	English	B	Science	Music
Tues	English	Geography	R	PE	Drama
Wed	English	Art	E	Games	
Thur	History	Science	A	English	Maths
Fri	English	Maths	K	PE	Music

A Think about

Write a sentence to answer each question.

1 What lesson is at 10.45 on Thursday?
2 How long is the geography lesson on Tuesday?
3 How many mornings each week is there a maths lesson?
4 How long is break?

B Vocabulary

> **Compound** words are made up of two words joined together.
> e.g.   time + table = **timetable**

Find two compound words beginning with:

a rain	b night	c fire	d book
e road	f house	g eye	h water

Use a dictionary to help you.

C Talk about

People use bus timetables to find out when buses are leaving and what time they will arrive.

Here is a bus route from London to Manchester.

Here is the bus timetable.

London	7.30	10.20	14.45
Oxford	9.15	12.05	16.30
Birmingham	10.30	13.20	17.45
Manchester	12.30	15.20	19.45

1 What time is the first bus that leaves London?

2 What time does it arrive in Manchester?

3 Where can you catch a bus at 12.05?

4 If you catch the bus in Birmingham at 10.30, what time will you arrive in Manchester?

5 How long does it take the bus to go from London to Oxford?

6 How long does it take the bus to go from Oxford to Birmingham?

7 How long does it take the bus to go from Birmingham to Manchester?

8 How long is the complete bus journey?

D Extra

Here is the route from Doncaster to Birmingham by the fast inter-city train. Write a timetable for the three trains that travel along this route.

1 Train A sets off at 11.00.

   Train B sets off at 15.00.

   Train C sets off at 17.00.

2 The journey from Doncaster to Sheffield takes 25 minutes.

3 The journey from Sheffield to Derby takes 45 minutes.

4 The journey from Derby to Birmingham takes 1 hour 15 minutes.

The Story of Gelert

In the time of Prince Llewelyn, the valleys below Snowdon were thickly clothed with forests, and the forests were full of wild animals. Foxes and wolves as well as stags and hares roamed there and, except for a hunting lodge in a forest clearing where the River Colwyn meets the River Glaslyn, there was no town or village for miles around.

Prince Llewelyn was very fond of hunting. He came to stay at the hunting-lodge with his servants and horses and hounds, and with him came his wife, Princess Joan, and their baby son. There was a nurse to look after the baby so that the Princess could go out hunting with her husband.

One day, they all set off into the forest to hunt stag, the Prince and the Princess on their horses, the servants on foot and the hounds trotting beside them eager for the chase. Only the nurse was left behind to look after the baby who was asleep in his cradle. And no sooner had the hunting party gone than the man who was courting the nurse came to take her off for a walk in the woods. The door of the house was left open.

Meanwhile, the hounds had picked up the trail of a stag. They were big dogs, faithful and brave, and the bravest and most faithful of all was Gelert. Llewelyn was very fond of Gelert, who never failed to be the first on the scent and the boldest in attacking the quarry. When the Prince noticed that today Gelert was not among the other hounds, he reined in his horse at once and asked if anyone had seen the dog.

'Gelert was with us until we crossed the last stream, my lord,' said one of the servants.

'I saw him going back by the way we came,' said another.

Princess Joan touched her husband's arm. 'Gelert must have gone back to the house,' she said anxiously. 'Can something be wrong there?'

At this, Llewelyn was worried too. He gave the order to abandon the hunt and to go back through the forest, the Prince and Princess cantering ahead on their horses. As they came in sight of the house, they saw Gelert come out and run towards them, wagging his tail. But when he came closer, the Princess gave a cry and sank, fainting, from her horse, for the dog was all smeared and dripping with blood.

Showell Styles

A Think about

Write a sentence to answer each question.

1 What were to be found in the valleys below Snowdon?

2 What was to be found where the River Colwyn met the River Glaslyn?

3 Why did Prince Llewelyn and Princess Joan take a nurse with them?

4 What animal's trail did the hounds pick up?

5 Why did the Prince order everyone back to the house?

6 Why did the Princess faint?

B Vocabulary

1 Explain the following phrases from the story in your own words.

    a   eager for the chase

    b   picked up the trail

    c   attacking the quarry

    d   reined-in his horse

    e   abandoned the hunt

2 Write the past tense of these verbs. You will find them in the story.

    a are   b come   c go

    d see   e give   f notice

C Talk about

1 How do you know that the nurse was not to be trusted?

2 Why was Llewelyn very fond of Gelert?

3 Why was Princess Joan sure that something was wrong?

4 When they saw Gelert covered in blood, what do you think the Prince and Princess thought had happened?

5 What do you think had happened in the house?

D Extra

Imagine you are Gelert.

You sense something is wrong and you go back to the hunting lodge.

What do you find?

What do you do?

Write and ending for the story.

How to Use this Book

The student book is divided into 15 units of work, which have been carefully written to gain a gradual progression in learning and building on learning across the whole year. The units of work include extracts and short texts covering a full range of fiction, poetry and non-fiction.

The units can be used over several lessons if necessary, and it is suggested that first of all, the students are allowed to read the whole text or extract before beginning to answer the questions.

Think About

These questions are designed to test the literal understanding of the text for all students, and can be completed as a written exercise.

Vocabulary

These activities pick up on some of the vocabulary the students have encountered in the text, in order to test their word knowledge and spelling patterns.

Talk About

These are a series of questions about the text which require the children to use their skills of deduction, inference and evaluation. Depending on the students' abilities and learning needs, the children could discuss in small groups or in a teacher-led whole class discussion, before they write their answers.

Extra

This is a longer written activity which allows students to respond to and extend their understanding of the text. Again, depending on students' abilities and learning needs, this could be introduced with a short whole-class or group discussion, and could be completed as independent work outside the lesson.